DEVOTIONS TO THE HOLY ANGELS

DEVOTIONS
to the
HOLY ANGELS

From Various Sources

AROUCA
PRESS

ISBN: 978-1-998492-01-5

Arouca Press
PO Box 55003
Bridgeport PO
Waterloo, ON N2J 0A5
Canada
www.aroucapress.com
Send inquiries to info@aroucapress.com

CONTENTS

DEVOTIONS
to the
HOLY
ANGELS[*]

* From the meditations of Henri-Marie Boudon (1624–1704), abbot, and spiritual author.

OFFERING TO THE HOLY ANGELS

O ALL YE HOLY ANGELS! WHO CONTEM-plate unceasingly the uncreated Beauty of the Divinity, in company with your ever glorious Queen—I, your unworthy servant, present and offer to you all the practices of this Month of October, consecrated to your glory, not only as a means of obtaining [*here specify your request*], but also as a reparation for my past ingratitude and that of all men. Deign to accept it, O amiable Spirits!, in union with the love and devotion of such Saints as were specially devout to you—and obtain for me to spend this time so fervently, that it may be the commencement of that angelic life which I hope to live for ever with you in Heaven. *Amen*.

A MEMORARE TO THE ANGELS

R EMEMBER—O HOLY ANGELS!—THAT Jesus, the eternal Truth, assures us that you "rejoice more at the conversion of one sinner, than at the perseverance of many just." Encouraged thereby, I, the most unworthy of creatures, humbly entreat you to receive me as your servant and make me unto you a cause of true joy. Do not—O blessed Spirit!— reject my petition; but graciously hear and grant it. *Amen*.

I. THE CREATION OF THE ANGELS

ANTICIPATE ALL TIME—PENETRATE THE eternal years—and contemplate in wonder and amazement that eventful moment in which the Deity, coming forth from that inaccessible light in which He dwelt, spoke the word and created the Angels. Wonderful Spirits! Their perfections are like the vast and unfathomable sea. Beings incomprehensible—they sow forth in their celestial endowments the omnipotence, love, and wisdom of their Almighty Maker. They are incorruptible in their celestial endowments, the omnipotence, love, and wisdom of their Almighty Maker. They are incorruptible in their nature—endowed with wonderful knowledge—clothed with divine purity, consumed with celestial love. Their power is amazing—their beauty so ravishing, that St. Bridget says the appearance of one alone of them to mortal man would occasion immediate death. Their sanctity exceeds that of all the Saints, since they have been replenished with the divine unction and have never contracted actual stain. Their charity is exceedingly great, since they have received more of that sacred fire which, according to St. John, is the essence of the Godhead, than all other creatures. This is saying much, and yet it conveys but a faint idea of the perfection of these celestial Spirits. Let us, while we confess their greatness, bless the hand of Him who made them and commence this holy exercise as they began their angelic course, saying:

Practice: The *Te Deum*.

Aspiration for the Day: Holy, Holy, Holy, Lord God of Sabaoth! The Heavens and the Earth are full of Thy glory! Glory be to the Father! — Glory be to the Son! — Glory be to the Holy Ghost!

II. THE ANGELS OF THE FIRST CHOIR

THOUGH ALL THE BLESSED SPIRITS ARE commonly styled Angels. It is to those of the First Choir that the appellation strictly belongs. They are charged with the execution of the divine ordinances and are appointed the guardians of men. Humility is the virtue particularly ascribed to them—for, though the least among the Choirs, yet they see their celestial companions without desiring their greater and more excellent endowments. Let us, like them, love to occupy the lowest place, especially when placed therein by Divine Providence, and to behold with joy the preference given to others.

Practice: Three Acts of Humility, interior or exterior.

Aspiration: "Who is like God?"

III. THE ARCHANGELS: SECOND CHOIR

THE ARCHANGELS ARE DISTINGUISHED from the Angels by the greater importance of their functions. They are supposed to be the guardians of all invested with authority in Church and State—and are remarkable for their love and care of men. Let us imitate them, doing our neighbor all the good we can and invoking in his behalf these blessed Spirits.

Practice: Two Acts of Charity, with great affection.

Aspiration: Holy Archangels! Pray for us.

IV. THE PRINCIPALITIES: THE THIRD CHOIR

THE *PRINCIPALITIES*, WHO FORM THE Third Choir, are charged to watch over Empires, Provinces, Dioceses, *etc.* and to avert from them the effects of the Divine wrath. They are also appointed to transmit to the Angels of the last two Choirs the orders of the Most High. Purity of intention is the virtue ascribed to them, for in their high functions they never seek but the honour and interest of God alone. Let us imitate them. It is the intention which stamps the action with merit or demerit.

Practice: In all you do and say, seek the greater glory of God. Refer all to this end.

Aspiration: O Holy Spirits! May we, like you, seek God, for God alone.

V. THE POWERS: THE FOURTH CHOIR

THE ANGELS OF THIS CHOIR HAVE received from God unlimited sway over the wicked Spirits; they are endowed with great intelligence, so as to be able to discover their schemes and plans for our destruction. Their power is so amazing that one alone of them would be able to destroy all the infernal host. It is well to invoke them in temptation: but to merit their assistance we must take care to avoid the occasions of sin.

Practice: Resist the attacks of vice and passion; frequently make acts of diffidence in self and confidence in God; combat your evil inclinations.

Aspiration: Lord! Send Thy Angels to assist us.

VI. THE VIRTUES: THE FIFTH CHOIR

E NERGY AND STRENGTH ARE ATTRIBUTED to the *Virtues*. They have dominion over the elements; all nature is subjected to their control. Hence they can raise or appease the tempest. We may profitably invoke them in unforeseen accidents, sickness, *etc*. We may also have recourse to them for that strength necessary to lead a penitential life and root out the inclinations of depraved nature.

Practice: Visit the Holy Sacrament to obtain grace to overcome your evil inclinations, *etc.*

Aspiration: Holy Virtues! Strengthen and fortify us.

VII. THE DOMINATIONS: THE SIXTH CHOIR

Z EAL FOR THE DIVINE GLORY DISTIN- guishes the *Dominations*. They are consumed by their yearning for the interests of God—their principal office is to manifest His will. We, too, ought to be interested in all that concerns the honour of this ever adorable Being, such as the conversion of sinners, the perfection of the just, the decoration of altars. We should also beg of God to manifest His will to us by these blessed "Intelligences"—and then take care to fulfill it scrupulously, as being the shortest way to perfection and sanctity.

Practice: Give practical proof of your zeal for the glory of God; do something for His reign in souls, as instructing the ignorant, *etc.*

Aspiration: Holy Dominations! Animate us with your zeal.

VIII. THE THRONES: THE SEVENTH CHOIR

THE SCRIPTURE SAYS OF THE LORD, THAT He is seated on *Thrones*. Hence these blessed Spirits are called Angels of Peace—being calm, tranquil, immovable. Ask them for that peace of soul which is the fruit of a good conscience. Invoke their aid for such as are prone to hatred, passion, and impatience, and, after their example, be you yourself meek, calm, and peaceful with all.

Practice: In the morning, dispose yourself to great sweetness and patience — and every hour make an act thereof.

Aspiration: O Holy Thrones! Obtain "that divine peace, which surpasses all understanding, and keep our hearts and minds in Christ Jesus, our Lord."

IX. THE CHERUBIM: THE EIGHTH CHOIR

THESE BLESSED SPIRITS ARE SO MANY sacred fires, communicating the divine light to the other Choirs. They are employed continually in contemplating the beauty and other perfections of their great Creator and will share with us their admirable lights, if we but ask them and show ourselves in earnest, by the practice of recollection and prayer, the channel of Divine communications.

Practice: Spend this day in great silence and recollection; be occupied with the consideration of the Divine perfections; endeavor to "know God, and Him whom He has sent, Jesus Christ."

Aspiration: Ah! Blessed Cherubim! Teach us to pray.

X. THE SERAPHIM: THE NINTH CHOIR

THE SERAPHIM HOLDS THE FIRST PLACE among the celestial Hierarchies. Their characteristic is great and ardent love. Filled with that torrent of delights which runs with a strong stream from the throne of the Divinity, these blessed Spirits are always in ecstasy. We should often form acts of divine love and beg of Jesus, the King of Love, through Mary, the Mother of Holy Love, and the Blessed Seraphim, the Spirits of Love, never to let this sacred fire be extinguished in our souls.

Practice: Try to become a Seraph in love; let this be your habitual disposition. Love, and do what you will. Ask this great gift fervently.

Aspiration: Oh! Blessed Seraphim! Make us love.

XI. THE ANGELS OF THE ANCIENT PEOPLE OF GOD

LET US THIS DAY VENERATE THE ANGELS who guarded the ancient people of God. Abraham, Isaac, Jacob, and Moses, were often favoured with their visits. It was one of these blessed Spirits who gave the law on Mount Sinai and conducted the Israelites through the desert in the pillar of a cloud. The Saints of those times were so convinced of their continual protection that even when they gave no sensible proof of their presence, they attributed to them the success of their affairs. "It is the Angels of the Lord," said they, "who hath done this."

Practice: The *Benedicite* in thanksgiving for this protection of the Angels.

Aspiration: Holy Angels! "Leaders of the House of Israel" intercede for us.

XII. THE ANGELS WHO ADORED JESUS AT THE MOMENT OF HIS INCARNATION AND NATIVITY

LET US THIS DAY VENERATE THE ANGELS who adored Jesus at the moment of His Incarnation, and when He appeared in the flesh. No sooner did He assume our nature at Mary's *fiat*, than her room was filled with innumerable troops of these blessed Spirits, all vying with one another in adoring the Son and in greeting the Mother; and on that ever blessed night, when He appeared wrapped in swaddling clothes and was laid in a manger, they again descended and rended the air with "Glory be to God on high, and peace on earth to men of good will!"

Practice: In honour of these Angels say the *Gloria in excelsis.*

Aspiration: Glory be to God—honour to the Angels, and peace to men of good will!

XIII. THE ANGELS AS SERVANTS AND SUBJECTS OF THE BLESSED VIRGIN MARY

SCARCELY WAS IT ANNOUNCED TO THE heavenly Spirit that a Queen was "born to them", than they descended in myriads and hovered round her cradle in wonder and delight. They guarded her infant steps; they conveyed her to the Temple; they unceasingly continued their celestial cares, until, by means of the Incarnation, she became the temple of the Word, when their visits were so frequent that her little cottage became a species of Paradise. At Bethlehem, in Egypt, and at the Holy Sepulchre, they continued to wait on their blessed Queen, until, expiring under the wounds of holy love, they conducted her with celestial song through realms of light and presented her to the Lamb, casting their crowns before her throne, vowing her eternal love, obedience, and fidelity. If we love our blessed Mother, we cannot refuse to honour those by whom she is so much honoured.

Practice: In honour of the Blessed Virgin and the Angels, say three times the Anthem, *Ave Regina Cælorum, etc.*

Aspiration: O Mary! Queen of the Angels and of the holy Rosary, intercede for us!

XIV. LET US THIS DAY VENERATE THE ANGELS WHO MINISTERED TO JESUS CHRIST AFTER HIS FAST IN THE DESERT

THE TIME BEING COME WHEN THE SAV-iour of men was to manifest Himself to Israel—having prepared for His mission by "a fast of forty days and forty nights, He was," says the Evangelist, "afterwards hungry, and Angels came and ministered to Him." Happy—thrice happy Spirits! Whom the Lord of Heaven and Earth, "He who gives food to the raven, when her young ones cry for meat—who opens His hand, and fills every living creature," permitted to minister to Him in His necessities. It rests with us to be sharers in their happiness, for Jesus is still upon earth in the persons of His poor—and what we do for them, He considers as done for Himself.

Practice: Give some alms in the spirit of these Angels ministering to our Lord.

Aspiration: Holy Angels, ministering Spirits to Jesus Christ, intercede for us.

XV. LET US DEVOTE THIS DAY TO THE VENERATION OF THE ANGELS WHO APPEARED AT THE SEPULCHRE OF JESUS

WE MAY PIOUSLY IMAGINE THAT AFTER the body of our crucified King was laid in the tomb, the holy Angels came and guarded it, completely awestruck at this, His annihilation, until "the morning of the Sabbath, when the Martyrs, on coming to the door of the sepulchre, found the stone rolled away, and an Angel sitting thereon, whose countenance was as lightning, and his garments like snow." This conduct of the Angels should make us like the great Saint Teresa, who was most assiduous in visiting Jesus in His holy Sacrament, the tomb of His love. He is there night and day, suffering with infinite patience the irreverences of some and the total forgetfulness of almost all.

Practice: A visit to the Holy Sacrament, to beg a great devotion towards it and the Angels.

Aspiration: Ah! Blessed Angels! Teach us to honour Jesus in the Sacrament of His love.

XVI. LET US THIS DAY HONOUR THE ANGELS WHO APPEARED AT THE ASCENSION OF JESUS CHRIST

THE TIME BEING COME WHEN JESUS WAS to pass out of the world and to ascend to His Father, He led His disciples to Olivet, and, having given them His last instructions, He was taken up into heaven, and a cloud took Him out of their sight. And as they continued to look after Him, two men stood by them clothed in white, who said, "You men of Galilee, why *stand* you looking up to heaven? This Jesus, whom you have seen ascend there will one day return." It is not by devotion merely speculative, as those Angels insinuated, that we are to prepare for this coming. We must pray, act, and suffer, lest we be found with our hands empty when the Lord will descend to judge us.

Practice: Examine for five minutes if your devotion be in accordance with the Spirit of God — whether it shows itself by subjection of the passions, *etc.*, or in mere external forms only.

Aspiration: O blessed Spirits render us adorers in spirit and in truth.

XVII. OUR GUARDIAN ANGELS

B LESSED FOR EVER BE THAT INFINITE goodness which, not content with all that it has done for us, has deputed an Angel to be our guide—and woe be to us if we are insensible to this favour. It is indeed true that "God has given His Angels charge over us"; that they are always at our side; that they bear us up in their hands" and lose not sight of us day or night. Let us be grateful to those blessed Guardians and, as St. Bernard recommends, show respect for their presence, affection for their services, confidence in their guardianship. Let each of us often say to his Guardian Angel, with sincere regret for past want of devotion—too late have I loved you, O good Angel!

Practice: The Litany of the Guardian Angel.

Aspiration: O blessed Angel! I love you and wish to love you more.

XVIII. THE ANGEL OF OUR PATRON SAINT

LET US THIS DAY HONOUR THE ANGEL Guardian of our Patron, as this blessed Spirit has done so much for his or her sanctification. It is gratifying to them that we show them honour; they will not fail to acknowledge it.

Practice: Visit the Angel of your Patron to thank him and beg his intercession.

Aspiration: Holy Angel of my Patron! I venerate you.

XIX. THE ANGELS OF OUR FAMILY & RELATIONS

HONOUR THE ANGELS OF YOUR FAMILY and Relations; they often render services which you would not receive from your own Angels, perhaps because of some advantage which is derived from some good which you do for those of whom they have charge.

Practice: A communion in honour of these Angels.

Aspiration: Holy Angels! I revere you.

XX. THE ANGELS OF OUR FRIENDS & BENEFACTORS

PAY PARTICULAR RESPECT TO THOSE HOLY Spirits who are entrusted with the guardian-ship of your friends and benefactors, knowing that the services which they render to you are often prompted by these blessed Angels. The Angel of your Confessor, being your best friend, deserves special devotion and affection.

Practice: Say nine Hail Marys in honour of these Angels.

Aspiration: Lord! Charge Thy Angels to keep us in all our ways!

XXI. THE ANGELS OF OUR CITY & KINGDOM

THAT GOD HAS APPOINTED CERTAIN Angels to watch over and defend Kingdoms and Provinces, we are assured of in the Book of Genesis. Towns and Cities too have their respective Angels. We ought often and earnestly to recommend these places to their guardian care and beg, while we thank them for past protection, so that they would arrest by their prayers the torrent of vice and immorality which so loudly demands vengeance.

Practice: Say the Rosary in honour of these Angels.

Aspiration: In sight of Thy Angels — O Lord! — will I sanctify Thy name.

XXII. THE ANGELS OF OUR PARISH

INVOKE THE ANGELS OF YOUR PARISH, that they may avert from it the wrath of the Most High, excited by the continual offences committed against Him. Father Le Fevre, first companion of St. Ignatius, used to invoke the Angels of the different places in which he preached, that they might dispose the people to profit by his sermons, *etc.*

Practice: Say the Litany of the Angels for the reign of God in your parish.

Aspiration: O Holy Angels! Preserve us from all evil, especially that of sin.

XXIII. THE ANGELS OF HERETICS & INFIDELS

SPEND THIS DAY IN MAKING REPARATION to the Angels for the ill return made for all their cares by Heretics and Infidels. The former blaspheme against them, whilst the latter are in total ignorance or disbelief of them.

Practice: Interiorly salute the Angels of all whom you meet.

Aspiration: May every creature praise the Angels.

XXIV. ST. RAPHAEL

THE NAME OF THIS BLESSED ANGEL SIG- nifies "cure" of God. He is according to his own testimony to Tobias, one of the seven Spirits who stand before the Throne of God. From having so safely conducted that good man on his journey to Rages, and the many helps afforded by him during his stay in that city, he should be invoked by travellers and voyagers, persons about to con- tract the sacred matrimonial engagement, as well as those engaged in trade and commerce. Indeed, all should beg his assistance, all being strangers and pilgrims upon earth and standing in a greater or lesser need of it.

Aspiration: O Angel of God, illumine, defend, and preserve me this day and for ever.

XXV. ST. GABRIEL

THIS BLESSED SPIRIT WAS THE AMBASSA- dor of the Most High when about to work the greatest of all His mysteries, the Incarnation of His Son; and he it was that revealed it to Dan- iel many ages before. He is supposed to have been the tutelary of the Holy Family—the Angel who invited the shepherds to the manger—who warned St. Joseph to flee to Egypt—and, in fine, he who consoled Jesus in His agony. His name, Gabriel, signifies "power of God". His peculiar grace is to imprint in hearts the knowledge and love of Jesus and Mary. Let us be devout to him, and he will render us this service so desirable.

Practice: Say, in honour of this blessed Angel, seven times his own words to the Blessed Virgin — Hail Mary, *etc.*

Aspiration: O "Angel of the Lord!", extend in all hearts the empire of Jesus and Mary.

XXVI. ST. MICHAEL

WHEN LUCIFER RAISED HIS REBELLIOUS head and sought to be like the Most High, Michael, the Prince of the Seraphim and the first of "the Seven Spirits who stand before the Throne", opposed his haughty pretensions and overthrew him in the contest. Saint Thomas supposes this blessed Spirit to be the breath of the Saviour which will destroy Antichrist. He is the patron of the Church—the protector of the dying—he, in fine, who on the last day will seize the trumpet and with a *Surgite Mortui*, "Arise, ye dead!", will arraign all men before the Judge of the living and the dead. He is, then, entitled to singular love and veneration.

Practice: Nine *Gloria Patris,* in honour to St. Michael, as Chief of the Nine Choirs.

Aspiration: O Holy Michael the Archangel! Defend us in the combat, lest we perish in the Day of Judgment.

XXVII. THE ANGELS OF
BAD & IGNORANT CATHOLICS

THAT THERE ARE NUMBERS WHO BELONG to the one fold of Jesus Christ unmindful of their duty to those Holy angels whom they know to be their guardians and protectors—many more altogether ignorant of this consoling truth—is as undeniable as it is afflicting. Let us this day supply their deficiency by our homage and respect.

Practice: Assist at Mass in honour of these Angels.

Aspiration: For all who despise or forget you, I love and venerate you, holy Angels.

XXVIII. THE ANGELS WHO VISIT &
CONSOLE THE SOULS IN PURGATORY

THE CHARITY OF THE ANGELS DOES NOT end with our existence here: if condemned after death to the purifying flames of Purgatory, they visit and console us in a manner which considerably diminishes the sense of suffering. They have often appeared to persons on earth to incite them to relieve by prayers and good works the souls detained in Purgatory.

Practice: Sacrifice something at meals in honour of these Angels.

Aspiration: Holy Angels, I thank you.

XXIX. THE ANGELS WHO
FAVOURED PARTICULAR SAINTS

LET US CONSECRATE THIS DAY TO THOSE blessed Spirits who specially favoured some of the Saints; as the Angels who released St. Peter from his prison and revealed to St. John the secrets of the future; those who gave the monastic rule to St. Pachomius; who imprinted the holy stigmas in the body of St. Francis; who wounded the heart of St. Teresa; and those who gave the Holy Communion to St. Stanislaus, who conversed with St. Rose and conferred on St. Thomas the gift of perfect chastity. Thus we will please those great servants of God and obtain their intercession.

Practice: Three spiritual communions in honour of these Angels.

Aspiration: O all ye holy Saints and Angels, intercede for us!

XXX. ALL THE ANGELS,
BECAUSE THEY ASSIST US IN DEATH

WE ARE BORN BUT TO LIVE, WE LIVE but to die, and our lot for eternity depends on the manner in which we breathe our last. We ought, then, to "make for ourselves friends", for that critical moment, of the Holy Angels, by a true, sincere, and persevering devotion to them. If we do it, it is then, indeed, they will show how they loved us.

Practice: Say the beads of the Holy Angels.

Aspiration: O holy Angels — Spirits of God! — pray for us, now and at the hour of our death — *Amen.*

XXXI. ALL THE ANGELS, BECAUSE THEY WILL
CONTRIBUTE TO OUR HAPPINESS IN ETERNITY

WHEN THIS WORLD SHALL HAVE PASSED away, when the earth and all that is in it shall have been burnt up, and the elements melted with fire, when, in fine, the Son of Man shall appear in a cloud to judge the living and the dead, the Angels, at His command, having separated the good from the bad, will encompass the former as a tower of defence against the evils which will cause the latter to exclaim: "Mountains fall upon us! Hills cover us!" And when the final sentence seals man's eternal doom, and the Supreme Arbiter, having locked on their respective inmates the gates of heaven and hell, has flung the keys into the ocean of eternity, these blessed spirits will seat us down at the table of the Lamb, rejoicing that our sorrow is changed into joy, and that the days of our mourning are ended. Let us love these holy Angels, but let us love them perseveringly. Perseverance crowns the work. If they deserved our homage yesterday, they as well and better deserve it to-day.

Practice: Excite others to be devout to the Angels.

Aspiration: Alleluia! Salvation to our God that sits upon the Throne; and may all His Angels say, *Amen.*

FEAST OF ALL SAINTS

O BLESSED SPIRITS! OUR GUARDIANS AND intercessors, your unworthy servant, grateful for the favours received from you during this holy month, come to present to you my warmest thanks on this Feast of the Saints, your blessed companions in glory, and as some mark of sorrow for past neglect—and of present love and respect—I offer you the little crown made of the pious practices performed during this month in your honour. Deign to accept it, O holy Angels! And obtain for us of God, through Jesus, His Incarnate Word, and

Mary, your august Queen, that persevering in the good resolutions where with He has inspired us now, we may eternally contemplate with you the Unfading Beauty whom we bitterly regret "having loved too late."

TE DEUM LAUDAMUS

We praise Thee, O God; we confess Thee, O Lord.
Te Deum laudamus: te Dominum confitemur.

Thee the eternal Father all the earth doth worship.
Te aeternum Patrem omnis terra veneratur.

Thee the Angels, and all the Powers,
Tibi omnes Angeli; tibi caeli et universae Potestates;

Thee the Cherubim and Seraphim proclaim
without ceasing.
Tibi Cherubim et Seraphim incessabili voce proclamant:

Holy, Holy, Holy, Lord God of Sabaoth.
Sanctus, Sanctus, Sanctus, Dominus Deus Sabaoth.

The heavens and the earth are full of the majesty
of Thy glory.
Pleni sunt caeli et terra maiestatis gloriae tuae.

Thee the glorious choir of Apostles,
Te gloriosus Apostolorum chorus,

Thee the numerous train of Prophets,
Te Prophetarum laudabilis numerus,

Thee the white robed army of Martyrs doth
praise.
Te Martyrum candidatus laudat exercitus.

Thee the holy Church throughout the world
confesses.
Te per orbem terrarum sancta confitetur Ecclesia,

The Father of immense majesty,
Patrem immensae maiestatis:

The venerable, true and only Son,
Venerandum tuum verum et unicum Filium;

The Holy Ghost, the Paraclete,
Sanctum quoque Paraclitum Spiritum.

Thou art the King of Glory, O Christ.
Tu Rex gloriae, Christe.

Thou art the eternal Son of the Father,
Tu Patris sempiternus es Filius.

Who when about to deliver man didst not abhor
a Virgin's womb.
*Tu ad liberandum suscepturus hominem, non horruisti
Virginis uterum.*

Thou having overcome the sting of death, hast
opened to believers the kingdom of heaven.
Tu, devicto mortis aculeo, aperuisti credentibus regna caelorum.

Thou sittest at the right hand of God, in the glory
of the Father.
Tu ad dexteram Dei sedes, in gloria Patris.

We believe Thee to be the Judge to come.
Iudex crederis esse venturus.

We therefore pray to Thee to help Thy
servants, whom Thou hast redeemed
by Thy Precious Blood.
*Te ergo quaesumus, tuis famulis subveni: quos pretioso
sanguine redemisti.*

Let them be numbered with Thy Saints in
eternal glory.
Aeterna fac cum sanctis tuis in gloria numerari.

Lord, save Thy people and bless Thy inheritance,
Salvum fac pópulum tuum, Dómine, et bénedic hæreditáti tuæ.

And govern and exalt them for ever and ever.
Et rege eos, et extólle illos usque in ætérnum.

Every day we bless Thee.
Per síngulos dies benedícimus te.

And we praise Thy name for ever and ever.
Et laudámus nomen tuum in saeculum, et in saeculum saeculi.

Vouchsafe, O Lord, to preserve us to-day without sin.
Dignáre, Dómine, die isto sine peccáto nos custodíre.

Have mercy on us, O Lord, have mercy on us.
Miserére nostri, Dómine, miserére nostri.

Let Thy mercy, O Lord, be upon us, according as
we have hoped in Thee.
*Fiat misericórdia tua, Dómine, super nos, quemádmodum
sperávimus in te.*

In Thee, O Lord, have I put my trust; let me not
be confounded for ever.
In te, Dómine, sperávi: non confúndar in ætérnum.

AVE REGINA CAELORUM

Hail, O Queen of Heaven enthroned.
Ave, Regina Caelorum,

Hail, by angels mistress owned.
Ave, Domina Angelorum:

Root of Jesse, Gate of Morn
Salve, radix, salve, porta

Whence the world's true light was born:
Ex qua mundo lux est orta:

Glorious Virgin, Joy to thee,
Gaude, Virgo gloriosa,

Loveliest whom in heaven they see;
Super omnes speciosa,

Fairest thou, where all are fair,
Vale, o valde decora,

Plead with Christ our souls to spare.
Et pro nobis Christum exora.

THE BENEDICITE

Or, CANTICLE OF THE HEBREW CHILDREN

All ye works of the Lord, bless the Lord,
    praise and extol him for ever.
Bless the Lord, ye Angels of the Lord,
    ye heavens bless the Lord.
All ye waters that are above the heavens,
    bless the Lord.
All ye powers of the Lord, sun and moon,
    bless the Lord.
Stars of heaven, bless the Lord.
Showers of dew, bless the Lord.
All Spirits of God, bless the Lord.
Fire and heat, bless the Lord.
Cold and summer, bless the Lord.
Dews and hoar-frost, bless the Lord.
Frost and cold, bless the Lord.
Ice and snow, bless the Lord.
Lightning and clouds, bless the Lord.
Let the earth bless the Lord; let it praise and
    magnify Him for ever.
Mountains and hills, bless the Lord; all things
    that spring in the earth, bless the Lord.
Bless the Lord, ye fountains; seas and rivers,
    bless the Lord; whales, and all that move
    in the waters, bless the Lord; bless the Lord
    all ye fowls of the air.
Beasts and cattle, bless ye the Lord, ye sons of
    men, bless the Lord.
Let Israel bless the Lord, let it praise and extol
    Him for ever.
Priests of the Lord, bless the Lord; servants of
    the Lord, bless the Lord.

Spirits and souls of the Just, bless the Lord;
    ye holy and humble of heart, bless the Lord.
Ananias, Azarias, Misael, bless the Lord;
    praise and extol Him for ever.
Let us bless the Father, and the Son, and the Holy
    Ghost; let us praise and magnify Him for ever.
Blessed art Thou Lord in the firmament of
    Heaven, and praised and glorified and
    extolled for ever.

GLORIA IN EXCELSIS

GLORY BE TO GOD ON HIGH, AND PEACE ON earth to men of good will. We praise Thee, we bless Thee, we adore Thee, we glorify Thee, we give Thee thanks for Thy great glory. O Lord God, Heavenly King, God the Father Almighty, Lord Jesus Christ, Thy only begotten Son, Lord God, Lamb of God, Son of the Father, who takest away the sins of the world, receive our prayer; who sitteth at the right hand of the Father, have mercy on us! For Thou alone art holy, Thou alone art Lord, Thou alone art most high in the glory of God the Father. *Amen*.

LITANY
OF THOSE SAINTS WHO HAVE BEEN
SPECIALLY FAVOURED BY THE ANGELS

Lord, *have mercy on us.*
Christ, *have mercy on us.*
Lord, *have mercy on us.*
Christ, *hear us.*
Christ, *graciously hear us.*
God, the Father of Heaven, *have mercy on us.*
God the Son, Redeemer of the World,
   have mercy on us.

God the Holy Ghost, *have mercy on us.*

Holy Trinity, One only God, *have mercy on us.*

Holy Mary, who hast been saluted by the
Archangel Gabriel, *pray for us.*

St. Joseph, who received the divine commands
by Angels, *pray for us.*

St. Peter, delivered from captivity by an Angel,
pray for us.

St. John, taught sublime secrets by an Angel,
pray for us.

SS. Gregory & Philip Neri, whose charity to the
poor caused the Angels to appear among them,
when you administered relief to their wants,
pray for us.

SS. Nicholas & Martin, whom the angels gratified
at death with heavenly music, *pray for us.*

St. Pachomius, who received by an Angel a rule for
the religious whom you governed, *pray for us.*

St. Francis, who received the stigmas of the Passion
by a Seraph, *pray for us.*

St. Wenceslaus, whom the Angels visibly
protected in battle, *pray for us.*

SS. Raymond & Stanislaus, who are said to have
received the Holy Eucharist by the ministry
of Angels, *pray for us.*

St. Thomas Aquinas, who received the gift of
chastity through the agency of an Angel,
pray for us.

St. Isidore, whom the Angels assisted at work to fur-
nish you with more time for prayer, *pray for us.*

St. Camillus, protected by Angels in your journeys,
pray for us.

St. Mary Magdalene, who learned the Resurrection
of Jesus from Angels, *pray for us.*

St. Catherine of Siena, espoused by Jesus Christ
in presence of the Angels, *pray for us.*

SS. Agnes & Cecilia, protected by Angels, *pray for us.*

St. Francis, who often conversed with, and received
from your good Angel innumerable favours,
pray for us.

St. Catherine of Sweden, whose soul at death was
received by Angels, *pray for us.*

St. Teresa, the transformation of whose heart with
Divine love was accomplished by an Angel,
pray for us.

St. Rose of Lima, who, in recompense of your
purity, enjoyed the familiarity of your Angel,
pray for us.

O all ye holy Saints who have been most devoted
to and favoured by the Angels, *pray for us.*

Lamb of God, who takest away the sins of the world,
pardon us, O Lord.

Lamb of God, who takest away the sins of the world,
hear us, O Lord.

Lamb of God, who takest away the sins of the world,
have mercy on us.

Lord hear my prayer,
And let my supplication come to Thee.

PRAYER

O GOD! WHO WITH WONDERFUL ORDER
hast regulated the functions of angels and
of men, grant that those who always assist before
Thy throne in heaven may defend us here on
earth, through Jesus Christ, Thy Son, our Lord,
who livest and reignest with Thee in the unity
of the Holy Ghost, one God, world without end.
Amen.

THE BEADS OF THE HOLY ANGELS

Say on the Cross, the *Te Deum.*

Say on the Decades (Which may be five, seven, or nine, as time and devotion serve) the *Ave Maria* or *Gloria Patri* — and at the end of each Decade say, "O holy Angels! I love you and wish to love you more."

LITANY of the HOLY ANGELS

Lord, *have mercy on us!*
Christ, *have mercy on us!*
Lord, *have mercy on us!*
Christ, *hear us!*
Christ, *graciously hear us!*
God, the Father of Heaven, *have mercy on us!*
God the Son, Redeemer of the World,
    have mercy on us!
God the Holy Ghost, *have mercy on us!*
Holy Trinity, only One God, *have mercy on us!*
Holy Mary, Queen of Angels, *pray for us.*
St. Michael, *pray for us.*
St. Raphael, *pray for us.*
Holy Seraphim, *pray for us.*
Holy Cherubim, *pray for us.*
Holy Thrones, *pray for us.*
Holy Dominations, *pray for us.*
Holy Virtues, *pray for us.*
Holy Powers, *pray for us.*
Holy Principalities, *pray for us.*
Holy Archangels, *pray for us.*
Holy Angels, *pray for us.*

Blessed Spirits, who surround the Throne of God
and incessantly sing to Him, Holy! Holy!
Holy! Lord God of Sabbaoth, *pray for us.*

Who dissipate our darkness and illumine our minds,
pray for us.

Who announce to us divine things, *pray for us.*

Who have received from God the care of men,
pray for us.

Who incessantly contemplate the beauty of His
countenance, *pray for us.*

Who rejoice at the conversion of a sinner, *pray for us.*

Who rescued Lot out of Sodom, *pray for us.*

Who ascended and descended by the ladder of
Jacob, *pray for us.*

Who gave the law to Moses on Sinai, *pray for us.*

Who announced joy to man at the birth of Christ,
pray for us.

Who ministered to Jesus after His fast of forty days,
pray for us.

Who appeared at His sepulchre, *pray for us.*

Who spoke to His Disciples at His Ascension,
pray for us.

Who will accompany Him at His last coming,
pray for us.

Who assist us at the hour of death, *pray for us.*

Who release from Purgatory the Souls detained there,
pray for us.

Who perform miracles by the Divine Power,
pray for us.

Who preside over States and Monarchies, *pray for us.*

Who have delivered the friends of God from
many dangers, *pray for us.*

Who consoled the Martyrs in their torments,
pray for us.

Who specially protect Prelates and Rulers, *pray for us.*
All ye celestial Orders and Hierarchies, *pray for us.*
From all sin and danger, *preserve us, O Holy Angels!*
From the Devil's malice, *preserve us, O Holy Angels!*
From heresy and schism, *preserve us, O Holy angels!*
From eternal damnation, *preserve us, O Holy Angels!*
From a sudden death, *preserve us, O Holy Angels!*
Lamb of God, who takest away the sins of the world,
    pardon us, O Lord!
Lamb of God, who takest away the sins of the world,
    hear us, O Lord!
Lamb of God, who takest away the sins of the world,
    have mercy on us!
Lord, *hear our prayer!*
And let my supplication come to thee!

PRAYER

O GOD! WHO WITH WONDERFUL ORDER hast regulated the functions of angels and men, grant that those who always assist before Your throne in Heaven may defend our lives here on earth—through Jesus Christ, Thy Son, our Lord, who livest and reignest with Thee in the unity of the Holy Ghost, one God, world without end. *Amen.*

LITANY of the GUARDIAN ANGEL

Lord, *have mercy on us!*
Christ, *have mercy on us!*
Lord, *have mercy on us!*
Christ, *hear us!*
Christ, *graciously hear us!*
God the Father of Heaven, *have mercy on us!*
God the Son, Redeemer of Men, *have mercy on us!*
God the Holy Ghost, *have mercy on us!*
Holy Trinity, one God, *have mercy on us!*
Holy Mary, Queen of Heaven, *pray for us.*
Holy Angel, my Guardian, *pray for us.*
Holy Angel, my Protector in all dangers, *pray for us.*
Holy Angel, my defence in all afflictions, *pray for us.*

Holy Angel, my most faithful Lover, *pray for us.*
Holy Angel, my Preceptor, *pray for us.*
Holy Angel, my Guide, *pray for us.*
Holy Angel, Witness of all my actions, *pray for us.*
Holy Angel, my Helper in all my difficulties,
    pray for us.
Holy Angel, my Negotiator with God, *pray for us.*
Holy Angel, my Advocate, *pray for us.*
Holy Angel, lover of Chastity, *pray for us.*
Holy Angel, lover of Innocence, *pray for us.*
Holy Angel, most obedient to God, *pray for us.*
Holy Angel, Director of my Soul, *pray for us.*
Holy Angel, model of Purity, *pray for us.*
Holy Angel, model of Docility, *pray for us.*
Holy Angel, my Counselor in doubt, *pray for us.*
Holy Angel, my Guardian through life, *pray for us.*
Holy Angel, my Shield at the hour of death,
    pray for us.
Lamb of God! Who takest away the sins of the world,
    spare us, O Lord!
Lamb of God! Who takest away the sins of the world,
    hear us, O Lord!
Lamb of God! Who takest away the sins of the world,
    have mercy on us!

PRAYER

O GOD! WHO WITH UNSPEAKABLE PROVI-
dence vouchsafest to send Thy Angels to
be our Guardians, mercifully grant, that we, Thy
supplicants, may be always defended by their protection and enjoy their eternal society—through
Jesus Christ, Thy Son, our Lord, who livest and
reignest with Thee, in the unity of the Holy Ghost,
one God, world without end. *Amen.*

DEVOTION in HONOR
of
ST. MICHAEL
& the Nine Choirs of Angels

CALLED THE "ANGELIC CHAPLET"

The person begins with an act of contrition, kneeling, if opportunity serves, before an image of St. Michael. He then proceeds:

℣. Incline unto my aid, O God.

℟. O Lord, make haste to help me. Glory be to the Father, *etc.*

FIRST SALUTATION

Our Father: once; *Hail Mary*: 3×, to the first angelic choir.

¶ By the intercession of St. Michael and the heavenly choir of the Seraphim, may it please God to receive into our hearts the fire of His perfect charity. *Amen.*

SECOND SALUTATION

Our Father: once; *Hail Mary*: 3×, to the second angelic choir.

¶ By the intercession of St. Michael and the heavenly choir of the Cherubim, may God, in His good pleasure, grant us grace to abandon the ways of sin and follow the path of Christian perfection. *Amen.*

THIRD SALUTATION

Our Father: once; *Hail Mary*: 3×, to the third angelic choir.

¶ By the intercession of St. Michael and the sacred choir of the Thrones. May it please God to infuse into our hearts the spirit of true and sincere humility. *Amen.*

FOURTH SALUTATION

Our Father: once; *Hail Mary*: 3×, to the fourth angelic choir.

¶ By the intercession of St. Michael and the heavenly choir of the Dominations, may it please God to grant us grace to have dominion over our senses and to correct our depraved passions. *Amen.*

FIFTH SALUTATION

Our Father: once; *Hail Mary*: 3×, to the fifth angelic choir.

℣ By the intercession of St. Michael and the heavenly choir of the Powers may God vouchsafe to keep our souls from the wiles and temptations of the devil. *Amen.*

SIXTH SALUTATION

Our Father: once; *Hail Mary*: 3×, to the sixth angelic choir.

℣ By the intercession of St. Michael and the choir of the admirable heavenly Virtues, may it please God to keep us from falling into temptation, and may He deliver us from evil. *Amen.*

SEVENTH SALUTATION

Our Father: once; *Hail Mary*: 3×, to the seventh angelic choir.

℣ By the intercession of St. Michael and the heavenly choir of the Principalities, may it please God to fill our souls with the spirit of true and sincere obedience. *Amen.*

EIGHTH SALUTATION

Our Father: once; *Hail Mary*: 3×, to the eighth angelic choir.

℣ By the intercession of St. Michael and the heavenly Choir of Archangels, may it please God to grant us the gift to persevere in the faith and in all good works, that we may thereby be enabled to attain the glory of paradise. *Amen.*

NINTH SALUTATION

Our Father: once; *Hail Mary*: 3×, to the ninth angelic choir.

℣ By the intercession of St. Michael and the heavenly choir of all the Angels, may God vouchsafe to grant us their guardianship through this mortal life and after death a happy entrance into the everlasting glory of heaven. *Amen.*

Then say the *Our Father* four times in conclusion; the first to St. Michael, the second to St. Gabriel, the third to St. Raphael, the fourth to our Guardian Angel.
This exercise ends with the following anthem:

ANTHEM

M ICHAEL, GLORIOUS PRINCE, CHIEF AND champion to the heavenly host, guardian of the souls of men, conqueror of the rebel angels, steward of the palace of God under Jesus Christ; our worthy leader, endowed with superhuman excellence and virtue: vouchsafe to free us all from ill, who with full confidence have recourse to thee, and by thy incomparable protection enable us to make progress every day in the faithful service of our God.

℣. Pray for us, most blessed Michael, prince of the Church of Jesus Christ.

℟. That we may be made worthy of His promises.

PRAYER

A LMIGHTY AND ETERNAL GOD, WHO, IN Thine own marvelous goodness and pity, didst, for the common salvation of men, choose the glorious archangel Michael to be the Prince of Thy Church: make us worthy, we pray Thee, to be delivered by his beneficent protection from all our enemies, that, at the hour of our death, none of them may approach to harm us; rather do Thou vouchsafe unto us that, by the same archangel Michael, we may be introduced into the presence of Thy most high and divine majesty. Though the merits of the same Jesus Christ our Lord. *Amen.*

PIUS IX., AUG. 8 1851, GRANTED TO ALL THOSE WHO shall say this chaplet:

¶ An indulgence of seven years and seven quarantines

¶ One hundred days indulgence, every day by carrying this chaplet or kissing the metal.

¶ A plenary indulgence, once a month, to those who shall say this chaplet every day for a month, on usual conditions.

¶ A plenary indulgence. On the condition given above on:
Feast of the apparition of St. Michael, May 18.
The dedication of St. Michael, September 29.
St. Gabriel the archangel, March 18.
St. Raphael the archangel, October 24.
Holy guardian angels, October 2.

To gain these indulgences, a chaplet must be used, consisting of the Our Father nine times, with the Hail Mary three times after each Our Father, and the Our Father four times at the end, saying at the same time in order, the corresponding salutation, with the anthem and prayer, at the end. These chaplets by order of His Holiness, Feb. 4, 1877, must be blessed by a priest who has from the Holy See the general faculty of blessing beads, medals, *etc*.

PRAYER AGAINST SATAN
& the Rebellious Angels

PUBLISHED BY ORDER OF POPE LEO XIII

THE HOLY FATHER EXHORTS PRIESTS TO SAY THIS prayer as often as possible, as a simple exorcism to curb the power of the devil and prevent him from doing harm. The faithful also may say it in their own name, for the same purpose, as any approved prayer. Its use is recommended whenever action of the devil is suspected, causing malice in men, violent temptations, and even storms and various calamities. It could be used as a solemn exorcism (an official and public ceremony in Latin), to expel the devil. It would then be said by a priest, in the name of the Church, and only with the Bishop's permission.

✠ In the Name of the Father, and of the
Son, and of the Holy Ghost. *Amen.*

PRAYER TO
SAINT MICHAEL THE ARCHANGEL

M OST GLORIOUS PRINCE OF THE HEAV-
enly Armies, Saint Michael the Archangel,
defend us in our battle against principalities and
powers, against the rulers of this world of darkness,
against the spirits of wickedness in the high places
(Eph. 6:12). Come to the assistance of men whom
God has created to His likeness and whom He has
redeemed to a great price from the tyranny of the
devil. Holy Church venerates thee as her guardian
and protector; to thee; the Lord has entrusted the
souls of the redeemed to be led into heaven. Pray
therefore the God of Peace to crush Satan beneath
our feet, that he may no longer retain men captive
and do injury to the Church. Offer our prayers to
the Most High, that without delay they may draw
His mercy down upon us; take hold of "the dragon,
the old serpent, which is the devil and Satan", bind
him and cast him into the bottomless pit "so that
he may no longer seduce the nations" (Apoc. 20:2).

EXORCISM

I N THE NAME OF JESUS CHRIST, OUR GOD
and Lord, strengthened by the intercession of
the Immaculate Virgin Mary, Mother of God, of
Blessed Michael the Archangel, of the Blessed
Apostles Peter and Paul, and all the Saints, (and
powerful in the holy authority of our ministry),*

---

* Lay people omit this parenthesis.

we confidently undertake to repulse the attacks and deceits of the devil.

PSALM 67: God arises: His enemies are scattered, and those who hate Him flee before Him.

As smoke is driven away, so are they driven: as wax melts before the fire, so the wicked perish at the presence of God.

℣. Behold the Cross of the Lord, flee bands of enemies.

℟. He has conquered, the Lion of the tribe of Juda, the offspring of David.

℣. May Thy mercy, Lord, descend upon us.

℟. As great as our hope in Thee.

The crosses indicate a blessing to be given if a priest recites the Exorcism; if a lay person recites it, they indicate the Sign of the Cross to be made silently by that person.

W E DRIVE YOU FROM US, WHOEVER YOU may be, unclean spirits, all satanic powers, all infernal invaders, all wicked legions, assemblies, and sects; in the Name and by the power of Our Lord Jesus Christ, ✠ may you be snatched away and driven from the Church of God and from the souls made to the image and likeness of God and redeemed by the precious Blood of the Divine Lamb. ✠ Most cunning serpent, you shall no more dare to deceive the human race, persecute the Church, torment God's elect, and sift them as wheat. ✠ The Most High God commands you, ✠ He with whom, in your great insolence, you still claim to be equal; He who wants all men to be saved and to come to the knowledge of the truth" (I Tim. 2:4). God the Father commands you. ✠ God the Son commands you. ✠ God the Holy Ghost commands you. ✠ Christ, God's Word made flesh, commands you; ✠ He who to save our race outdone through your envy, "humbled Himself, becoming obedient even unto death" (Phil. 2:8); He who has built His Church on the firm rock and declared that the gates of hell shall not prevail against Her, because He will dwell with Her "all days even to the end of the world" (Matt. 28:20). The sacred Sign of the Cross commands you, ✠ as does also the power of the mysteries of the Christian Faith. ✠ The glorious Mother of God, the Virgin Mary, commands you; ✠ She who by her humility and from the first moment of her Immaculate Conception, crushed your proud head. The faith of the Holy Apostles Peter and Paul and of the other Apostles commands you. ✠ The blood of the Martyrs and the pious intercession of all the Saints commands you. ✠

Thus, cursed dragon, and you, diabolical legions, we adjure you by the living God, ✠ by the true God, ✠ by the holy God, ✠ by the God "who so loved the world that He gave up His only Son, that every soul believing in Him might not perish but have life everlasting" (St. John, III); stop deceiving human creatures and pouring out to them the poison of eternal damnation; stop harming the Church and hindering her liberty. Begone, Satan, inventor and master of all deceit, enemy of man's salvation. Give place to Christ in whom you have found none of your works; give place to the One, Holy, Catholic, and Apostolic Church acquired by Christ at the price of His Blood. Stoop beneath the all-powerful Hand of God; tremble and flee when we invoke the Holy and terrible Name of Jesus, this Name which causes hell to tremble, this Name to which the Virtues, Powers, and Dominations of heaven are humbly submissive, this Name which the Cherubim and Seraphim praise unceasingly repeating: Holy, Holy, Holy is the Lord, the God of Armies.

℣. O Lord, hear my prayer.
℟. And let my cry come unto Thee.
℣. May the Lord be with thee.
℟. And with thy spirit.

Let us pray. — God of heaven, God of earth, God of angels, God of Archangels, God of Patriarchs, God of Prophets, God of Apostles, God of Martyrs, God of Confessors, God of Virgins, God who has power to give life after death and rest after work, because there is no other God than Thee, and there can be no other, for Thou art the Creator of all things, visible and invisible, of whose reign there shall be no end, we humbly prostrate ourselves before Thy glorious Majesty, and we beseech Thee to deliver us by Thy power from all the tyranny of the infernal spirits, from their snares, their lies and their furious wickedness; deign, O Lord, to grant us Thy powerful protection and to keep us safe and sound. We beseech Thee through Jesus Christ Our Lord. *Amen.*

From the snares of the devil, deliver us, O Lord.

That Thy Church may serve Thee in peace and liberty, we beseech Thee to hear us.

That Thou may crush down all enemies of Thy Church, we beseech Thee to hear us.

(Holy water is sprinkled in the place where we may be.)

Imprimatur: ✠ Henri, O. M. I.
Vicar Apostolic of James Bay
Aug. 15, 1967

S AINT MICHAEL THE ARCHANGEL, DEFEND us in the battle; be our protection against the malice and snares of the Devil. May God restrain him, we humbly pray, and do thou, O prince of the heavenly host, by the divine power cast into hell Satan and all the other evil spirits who roam through the world seeking the ruin of souls. *Amen.*

Most Sacred Heart of Jesus; have mercy on us (3×).